MARIA
making pottery

Hazel Hyde

Sunstone Press
Santa Fe, New Mexico

Copyright © 1973 by Hazel Hyde

Photographs courtesy Museum of New Mexico: #4591, #30923, #30961, #44191, #50082, #50085, #55203, #68351, #68352, #68355, #73445, #73449.

All Rights Reserved. No part of this book may be reproduced in any form or by any electronic or mechanical means including information storage and retrieval systems, without permission in writing from the publisher, except by a reviewer who may quote brief passages in a review.

REVISED EDITION

Printed in the United States of America

Library of Congress Cataloging in Publication Data:

Hyde, Hazel.
  Maria making pottry.

  Bibliography: p. 28-31
  1. Martinez, Maria Montoya. 2. Pottery—20th century—New Mexico. I. Title.
NK4210.M289H92   1983   738'.092'4   83-5093
ISBN: 978-0-86534-156-2

Published by SUNSTONE PRESS
              Post Office Box 2321
              Santa Fe, NM 87504-2321 / USA
              (505) 988-4418 / *orders only* (800) 243-5644

3

This is a picture-story about Maria Martinez, perhaps the most famous of all Indian potters, and her husband Julian. I wrote this story in the early 1930s so that the children of my private school in New York City would learn about American Indians and the way they make their pottery.

4

The pottery at San Ildefonso pueblo is made by women and decorated by both men and women. In the picture, Julian, Maria's husband, is painting a pot while Maria polishes another.

5

6

But to begin at the beginning: Julian goes out to a hillside near San Ildefonso where he has found red clay that will make good pottery. He digs out as much as he can carry in the large piece of cloth he uses for that purpose and, throwing it over his shoulder, takes it back to Maria.

8

Maria kneels on a Navajo rug on the shady side of the house and sifts the clay onto a square of canvas laid flat on the ground. You will notice in the picture that there are two colors of clay on the canvas. The lighter color is bluer clay that they brought from the Jemez Mountains where there is another pueblo. This blue clay makes the pottery tougher so it does not break so easily.

10

Into the dry, sifted clay, Maria next puts water from the pail on the ground by her side. She puts in just a little water at a time and works it into the clay until she has a big ball of wet, sticky clay.

12

Maria then takes a handful of the moist clay and pats it between her hands until she has made a thin pancake of it.

14

When Maria has the mud pancake just the size and thickness she wishes, she pats it down into the bottom of a plate and turns up the edges all around the top. This is for the bottom of the pot. She leaves it in the plate until the pot is finished.

16

Maria then takes another lump of clay and rolls it between her hands until she has a roll long enough to reach around the edge she has turned up. She presses it against the inside edge of the base, making sure that it is evenly joined all the way around. She adds one roll on top of another until she has the bowl the height and size she wants it to be. As she shapes the pot, she wets her fingers so that the mud will not stick to them and so that she can smooth the rolls of clay together. When she has finished, you cannot see that the pot has been built up with rolls. Now the pot is put up against the side of the house to dry.

18

Just before the pot is dry, to make it still smoother, Maria takes a round stone and polishes it. After all the pots are entirely dry. Maria calls Julian and they go into the house to decorate them

20

After the pots are made and decorated, they have to be fired so that they will not break easily. First, Julian makes a fire out-of-doors and lets it burn until there is a good bed of coals. On the coals he puts tin cans or stones to support a grate which is used to hold the pots for firing. Next he puts the pots upside down on the grate, being careful to place them so that their sides do not touch. After they are all stacked, they are covered with pieces of tin or old broken pots so that they will be kept clean while the fire is burning. Cakes of dried sheep manure are placed all around the pile and all over the top of it until it is completely covered. Then Julian and Maria set fire to the pile of manure and watch it carefully. When it has burned long enough, Julian brushes the ashes away and carefully picks up the fired pots with sticks and places them on the ground in the sun to slowly cool.

22

After the ashes are dusted off, Maria again polishes the pots, finishing by rubbing them with the palm of her hand until they achieve the high glaze for which her work is famous. When enough pots have been completed, they are carefully packed on a large piece of calico or a cotton blanket and tied by the four corners into a bundle. Then women lift these bundles to the tops of their heads and carry them, as you see in the picture, to the main highway where the women place them on the ground and sit beside them hoping that passing travelers will stop and buy them.

24

When the day's work is finished, Maria and Julian put on their fiesta costumes and go to an Indian dance.

25

26

The selling of the pots by the roadside was very successful in the 1930s and was still being done in the 1940s. But after the highways became speedways, Maria's son, Popovi Da, built an adobe salesroom by the side of the road leading from Santa Fe to Taos. This enterprise was later abandoned. After that Maria's pots were sold by her son in his shop near one of the entrances to San Ildefonso.

27

Bibliography

Allen, Kenneth. "Camera Touring New Mexico, the Pottery Makers." *New Mexico Magazine*, Vol. 19, No. 3, March 1941, pp. 18-19.

Arnold, David L. "Pueblo Pottery, 2,000 Years of Artistry." *National Geographic*, Vol. 162, No. 5, November 1982, pp. 593-605.

Bacon, Lucy. "Indian Independence Through Tribal Arts." *New Mexico*, Vol. 10, No. 2, January 1932, pp. 11-13, 44.

Barry, John. *American Indian Pottery, An Identification and Value Guide.* Florence, AL: Books Americana, 1981.

Bennett, James O'Donnell. "Indian Potters Create Marvels at World Fair." *New Mexican*, July 16, 1934.

Brody, J.J. "Southwestern American Indian Pottery, A Living Tradition." *American Art & Antiques*, Vol. 2, No. 5, September-October 1979, pp. 110-117.

Bunzel, Ruth. *The Pueblo Potter, A Study of Creative Imagination in Primitive Art.* New York: Columbia University Press, 1930. Revised edition, New York: Dover, 1972.

Challem, Jack Joseph. "A Black Bowl from New Mexico." *New Mexico Magazine*, Vol. 58, No. 7, Sept.1980, pp. 14-21.

Chapman, Kenneth M. *The Pottery of San Ildefonso.* Albuquerque: University of New Mexico Press, 1970.

_____. "Roadside Shopping." *New Mexico Magazine*, Vol 14, No. 6, June 1936, p. 21.

Clark, Ann D. "Catholic Art Association Honors Mrs. Maria Martinez." *New Mexican*, August 26, 1960, p. 8.

Dittert, Albert E., and Plog, Fred. *Generations in Clay: Pueblo Pottery of the American Southwest.* Flagstaff, AZ: Northland Press, 1980.

Dutton, Bertha P. *Indians of the American Southwest.* Englewood Cliffs, NJ: Prentice-Hall, 1975.

_____. *Indians of the Southwest, Pocket Handbook.* Santa Fe, NM: Southwestern Association on Indian Affairs, 1963.

Eby, Maurice. "A Great Tradition in Pottery." *New Mexico Magazine,* Vol. 40, No. 4, April 1962, pp. 12-13.

_____. "The Hands of Maria." *New Mexico Magazine,* Vol 45, No. 8, August 1967, pp. 29-31.

"Fine Exhibit of Pottery." *El Palacio,* Vol. 8, No. 7/8, July 1920, p. 217.

Fine, Robert Ross. "The Legacy of Maria Martinez." *Santa Fean,* Vol. 8, No. 9, October 1980, pp. 30-34, front cover.

Fox, Nancy. "Poveda, a Signature of Maria Martinez." Archaeological Society of New Mexico Papers, No. 3, 1976, pp. 259-264.

Gilpin, Laura. "Maria Martinez, Potter of San Ildefonso." *New Mexico Magazine,* Vol. 51, No. 1/2, January-February 1974, p. 32.

"A Great Tradition in Pottery." *New Mexico Magazine,* Vol. 40, No. 4, April 1962, pp. 12-13.

Gridley, Marion E. "Art Out of the Earth." *New Mexico Magazine,* Vol. 12, No. 11, November 1934, p. 7.

_____. *Indians of Today.* 3rd ed. Chicago: Indian Council Fire, 1960.

Guthe, Carl E. *Pueblo Pottery Making: A Study of the Village of San Ildefonso.* New Haven: Yale University Press, 1925.

Harrison, Will. "State's Most Distinguished Woman Receives New Honor." *Rodeo de Santa Fe Souvenir Program,* 1954, p. 57.

Hodge, Zahrah Preble. "Maria Martinez, Indian Master Potter." *Southern Workman,* Vol. 62, No. 5, 1933, pp. 213-215.

Hyde, Hazel. *Maria Making Pottery.* Santa Fe, NM: Sunstone Press, 1973.

"Indian Woman's Rediscovery of Old Art Brings Renaissance of Famed Pottery." *New Mexican,* May 27, 1956, p. 7C.

Jacka, Jerry, and Gill, Spencer. *Pottery Treasures, The Splendor of Southwest Indian Art.* Portland, OR: Graphic Arts Center, 1976.

LaFarge, Oliver. *A Pictorial History of the American Indian.* New York: Crown, 1957.

Lemos, Pedro J. "The Household Arts of the Indian Pueblos." *El Palacio*, Vol. 16, No. 8, April 15, 1924, pp. 127-129.

Lyon, Dennis. "The Polychrome Plates of Maria and Popovi." *American Indian Art Magazine*, Vol. 1, No. 2, February 1976, pp. 76-79.

McGreevy, Susan Brown. *Maria: The Legend, The Legacy*. Santa Fe, NM: Sunstone Press, 1982.

"Maria and Julian Martinez." *School Arts*, Vol. 49, No. 3, November 1949, p. 100

"Maria Displays Her Pottery." Color cover of *New Mexico Magazine*, Vol. 33, No. 7, July 1955.

"Maria Given Award." *New Mexican*, December 28, 1969.

Maria Martinez - Obituary. *New Mexican*, July 21, 1980, p. A-1.

"Maria Martinez Receives Jane Addams Award During Ceremonies in Santa Fe." *New Mexican*, September 6, 1959.

"Maria, Potter-Teacher." *The Atom*, Vol. 1, No. 5, May 1964, pp. 12-15.

"Maria, the Famed New Mexico Potter." *New Mexican Pasatiempo*, March 14, 1971, p. D1.

"Maria: The Potter from San Ildefonso." *Artists of the Rockies*, Vol. —, No. 2, Spring 1974, pp. 20-24.

Marriott, Alice, *Maria of San Ildefonso*. Norman OK: University of Oklahoma Press, 1948. Reprinted, 1976.

Maxwell Museum of Anthropology. *Seven Families in Pueblo Pottery*. Albuquerque, NM: University of New Mexico Press, 1974.

Nelson, Mary Carroll, *Maria Martinez*. Minneapolis, MN: Dillon, 1972.

New Mexico Magazine. *New Mexico Magazine's The Indian Arts of New Mexico*. Santa Fe, NM: 1975.

Peterson, Susan. *The Living Tradition of Maria Martinez*. Tokyo, New York: Kodansha, 1977, 1982.

_____. *Maria Martinez: Five Generations of Potters*. Washington, DC: Smithsonian Institution, 1978.

_____. "Matriarchs of Pueblo Pottery." *Portfolio*, Vol. 2, No. 5, November/December 1980, pp. 50-55.

"Poh-we-ka (Little Blue Corn Flower)." *El Palacio*, Vol. 6, No. 7, March 22, 1919, p. 98.

"Pueblo New Mexico Pottery." *El Palacio*, Vol. 16, No. 10, May 15, 1924, p. 157.

Ray Manley's Collecting Southwestern Indian Arts and Crafts. Tucson, AZ: Ray Manley Photography Inc., 1979.

Roberts Kathaleen, ed. *Indians of New Mexico.* Santa Fe, NM: New Mexico Commerce and Industry Department, 1981?.

Simpich, Frederick. "New Mexico Melodrama." *National Geographic Magazine*, Vol. 73, No. 5, May 1938, pp. 529-569.

Spivey, Richard L. *Maria.* Flagstaff, AZ: Northland Press, 1979.

_____ . "Signed in Clay: Three Eras of Maria Martinez's Creativity Are Traced By Her Valued Signature." *El Palacio*, Vol. 86, No. 4, Winter 1980-81, pp. 8-9.

Stuart, Jozefa, Ashton, Robert, Jr. *Images of American Indian Art.* New York: Walker, 1977.

Toulouse, Betty. "Maria - The Right Woman at the Right Time." *El Palacio*, Vol. 86, No. 4, Winter 1980-81, pp. 3-7.

_____ . *Pueblo Pottery of the New Mexico Indians: Ever Constant, Ever Changing.* Santa Fe, NM: Museum of New Mexico Press, 1977.

Trucco, Terry. "Pond Lily Has Them Lining Up." *Art News.* Vol. 80, No. 2, February 1981, p. 26.

Underhill, Ruth. *Pueblo Crafts.* Washington, DC: U.S. Bureau of Indian Affairs, 1944.

Watkins, T.H. "Legacy of Hands." *American Heritage*, Vol. 29, No. 6, October 1978, pp. 36-37.

Wilks, Flo. "Maria Revisited." *New Mexico Magazine*, Vol. 54, No. 5, May 1976, pp. 30-32.

Wormington, H.M., and Arminta, Neal. *The Story of Pueblo Pottery.* Denver: Denver Museum of Natural History, 1951.

Zebrowski, Jeanne-Marie. "The Marketplace: What Pot? Ancient, Old or New Southwest Indian Ware." American Art & Antiques, Vol. 2, No. 5, September-October 1979, pp. 35, 126, 129-136.

www.ingramcontent.com/pod-product-compliance
Lightning Source LLC
Chambersburg PA
CBHW051706040426
42446CB00009B/1331

MARIA
making pottery

Hazel Hyde

Maria Martinez is the renowned late potter of San Ildefonso Pueblo in New Mexico whose pots were often given by President Lyndon Johnson to visiting heads of state. This book tells, in simple terms and photographs, how she produced her famous polished blackware. Maria's pots are in museums and private collections all over the world. Hazel Hyde originally composed a picture story similar to the current book about Maria Martinez in 1930 for the students in her private school in New York City to teach them about pottery making among American Southwestern Indians.

$12.95

Audra Kerr Brown

hush hush hush